''The God Flame Code''

''English''

St**AR**ing f**OR**th **IN**to **THE** Null **VOID, MY FRIENDS**.
Into the Null Void from whi<u>ch</u> **I** c**AM**e.
Where C**H**a**O**<u>s</u> Mayhem and Hav**O**c re**I**gns.
Wh<u>ic</u>h the twists and turn<u>s</u> of this re**A**l**M** leads
me Into the Never-Ending
SAVIng **HEAR**t of God's Eternal Flame.

Ever <u>c</u>hanging me, hardening me, purifying me
like a ball of clay.
Fired into the shape of claves.
Producing the Ps**ALM**s of His **WAYS**.

Noth**IN**g else co**U**ld His Will, His P**R**e**S**ence, H**I**s Soul
can tame.
Eve**N** before I was given a Na**M**e.
Wh**I**ch was guided by the Golden Light of the
all-knowning God'**S** Eternal Flame.

Which I follow to thi**S** Day.
By feeling **THE** flickering war**M**th produced by
God's Eternal Fl**A**me.
Knowing One Day on this Ea**R**th, for Time Immortal.
From Atom to Atom.
The Son of Man He will reign.
Placing the Prince of the Air, on the Eve of the
Morning Star, into the cell that is
Known as Hell.
Where Forever Lucfier, the proud rebel of
the Dawn, will remain.
For all time he will be.
Knowing One Day on this Earth, for Time Immortal,
he will **be** sealed by the raging firey wrath of
God's Eternal Flame.
Never aga**in** to roa**m** fr**ee**.
Una**ble** **ev**e**r** again sow th**e** s**ee**ds of d**e**struction
diss**e**nc**e** li**e**s and misd**ee**ds.
By locking him up and throwing away the k**e**y.
Keeping us sa**f**e from the devil ha**r**ming
you and m**e**.

For**ev**er wh**ere** Satan will b**e** cag**ed**.
For which according to His Will,
His Presence, His S**ou**l.
Ever since Time Immortal, He Will Reign.
By the shining bright beacon of Go**d**'s E**t**ernal Flame.
Gu**i**di**n**g us day by day.
Saving us fro**m** th**e** w**AGE** **s** **OF SIN AND DEATH**.
Being condemned into a exi**sta**nce of insanity
dar**kn**e**ss** and pain.
The eating of the f**r**uits of g**ood** a**n**d evil.
Ba**d** for us **in** every which way.
For **our bodies our spirits** and **OUR BRAIinS**.
And realizing by doing so.
Is making us weak sickly infirm and lame.
While **being** Nake**d** **a**nd afr**a**id.
Turning our **souls** imperfect flawe**d** and ash**amed**.
Paid to us **b**y our labors for th**e** Old Man.
Will no longer rem**a**in.

Given to us with His Compassionate Sacrificial
Never-En**di**ng Under**s**tanding
Loving **Grace**.
By the flickering rays of God's Eternal Flame.
Back forth **in**to **the** Null **Void** which I came.
When you leave this realm and the helm
of the Null Void's ways.
Which is always in flux by the influential
tides that flow to and from its waves.
While passing through The Null Void,
Being Burnt up and consumed by
God's Eternal Lasting Flames.
Where which you will stand and where
you will always forever
remain.

''**The God Flame Code**''

''Greek''

Κοιτάζοντας μπροστά στο άδ**ει**ο κενό, φίλοι μου.
Στο **ά**δε**ι**ο κενό από το οποίο ήρθα.
Εκεί όπου βα**σι**λεύουν **το** χάος, ο όλεθρος **κ**αι
το πανδαιμόνιο.
Του οποίου οι ανατροπ**ές** και α**ν**αποδιές με
οδηγούν στην ατελείωτη λυτρωτική καρδιά
της Αιώνιας **Φ**λόγας του Θεού.
Πάντα με αλλά**ζει**, με σκ**λ**ηραίν**ει**, **μ**ε εξαγνίζει
σαν κ**ο**μμάτι από πηλό.
Παίρνοντας σχήμα γαρίφαλο**υ**.
Δημιουργώντας τις ψαλμωδίες των τρόπων του.
Τίποτα άλλο δεν θα μπορούσε να δαμάσει η
Θέλησή Του, η Παρουσία Του, τη Ψυχή Του.
Ακόμη και πριν μου δώσουν όνομα.
Από το Χρυσό Φως του παντογνώστη Θεού.
Αιώνια φλόγα.

Την οποία ακολουθώ μέχρι και σήμερα.
Νιώθοντας την παλλώμενη ζεστασιά που
παράγεται από την Αιώνια Φλόγα του Θεού.
Γνωρίζοντας πως μια μέρα σε αυτή τη Γη,
κατά την αιωνιότητα.
Από άτομο σε άτομο.
Ο Υιός του Ανθρώπου θα βασιλέψει.
Τοποθετώντας τον πρίγκηπα του αέρα,
κατά την Παραμονή του Πρωινού Άστρου,
στο κελί που είναι γνωστό ως Κόλαση.
Εκεί που θα παραμείνει ο παντοτινός Εωσφόρος,
ο περήφανος επαναστάτης της Αυγής.
Θα παραμείνει για πάντα.
Γνωρίζοντας πως μια μέρα σε αυτή τη Γη,
κατά την αιωνιότητα, θα είναι
σφραγισμένος από τη μαινόμενη πύρινη οργή
της Αιώνιας Φλόγας του Θεού.
Ποτέ ξανά να περιπλανηθεί ελεύθερος.
Ανίκανος να σπείρει ποτέ ξανά τους σπόρους
της καταστροφής, διχόνοια, ψέματα και
παραπτώματα.
Κλειδώνοντάς τον και πετώντας μακριά το κλειδί.
Κρατώντας μας ασφαλείς από τον διάβολο
που μας βλάπτει.

Για πάντα εκεί που θα εγκλωβιστεί ο Σατανάς.
Όπου σύμφωνα με το Θέλημά Του, την
Παρουσία Του, την Ψυχή Του.
Από την αρχή της αιωνιότητας, θα βασιλέψει.
Με το λαμπερό και φωτεινό φως της Αιώνιας
Φλόγας του Θεού.
Το οποίο μας καθοδηγεί μέρα με τη μέρα.
Σώζοντάς μας από την αμαρτία και τον θάνατο.
Καταδικασμένος σε μια ύπαρξη
παραφροσύνης, σκότους και πόνου.
Η βρώση των καρπών του καλού και του κακού.
Κακό για εμάς από κάθε άποψη.
Για το σώμα, το πνεύμα και τον εγκέφαλό μας.
Και συνειδητοποιούμε.
Ότι μας κάνουν αδύναμους, ανήμπορους
και κουτούς.
Ενώ είμαστε γυμνοί και φοβισμένοι.
Κάνουν τις ψυχές μας ατελείς, ελαττωματικές
και ντροπιασμένες.

Μας δώθηκε μέσα από τους κόπους μας για
αυτόν. Δεν θα παραμείνει πια.
Μας δόθηκε με την κατανοητική, ατελείωτη
και συμπονετική εύνοια Του.
Με τις τρεμουλιασμένες ακτίνες της Αιώνιας
Φλόγας του Θεού.
Πίσω στο άδειο κενό από το οποίο ήρθα.
Όταν αφήσεις αυτό το βασίλειο και τα ηνία
του κενού.
Το οποίο είναι πάντα σε κίνηση από τις
παλίρροιες που ρέουν από και προς τα κύματά του.
Περνώντας μέσα από το άδειο κενό,
Έχοντας καεί και εξαντληθεί από τις Αιώνιες και
Διαρκείς Φλόγες του Θεού.
Στις οποίες θα είσαι και για πάντα θα παραμείνεις.

SIC is in the beginning of the poem three times.
SIC is a phonetic spelling variation of the number six (6).
Which is representing the Number of the Beast (666) Six Hundred Sixty Six.

Found in the Book of Revelation Chapter 13 verse 18 (Revelation 13:18) in the New
Testament section of the Holy Bible.
The method of changing letters phrases and names into numbers is known as gematria.
Six is the number of the First Man (Adam) and the sign of incompletion corruption
sickness and flawed imperfection.

Reference sources from internet websites:

https://www.biblegematria.com/the-number-of-the-beast.html
https://web.library.yale.edu/cataloging/hebraica/about-gematria

English Gematria Calulator found online at:
https://www.gematrix.org/

AR OR IN THE VOID, MY FRIENDS?
Are you in the Void, my friends?

Revelation Chapter Three Verse Sixteen (Revelation 3:16) in the Holy Bible.
So then because thou art lukewarm, and neither cold nor hot, I will spue thee out of
my mouth.

Hot or cold, but be never luke warm.
You either are alive or dead.
We may be physically alive.
But inside all of us, The Null Void has us in its cold hard deafing chaotic grasp.
There is no such thing as being half-dead or half-alive.
Only the internal ignition of God's Eternal Flame (like a physician who treats the
sick
[They that are whole have no need of a physician; but they that are sick. I am not
come to call the righteous, but sinners, to repentance] {Luke Chapter Five Verses
Thirty-One to Thirty-Two.
5:31-32 from The Holy Bible}) will bring us out from our lost darkend chaotic
spiritual emotional and mental states.
Preventing us from wandering The Null Void like astronauts/cosmonauts floating
infinitely and helplessly in the hostile lifeless enviroment of outer space.
Without the pull of gravity Towards God's Eternal Flame and of His Eternal Grace.

Reference sources from internet websites:

https://biblia.com/bible/niv/luke/5/31-32
https://www.openbible.info/topics/the_great_physician
https://www.bible.com/bible/compare/REV.3.15-16
https://www.biblegateway.com/passage/?search=Revelation%203%3A15-17&version=NIV
https://www.bibleref.com/Revelation/3/Revelation-3-16.html
https://biblehub.com/revelation/3-16.htm

I AM WHOO I AM:

I AM WHO I AM!

Found in Exodus Chapter Three (3) Verse fourteen (14) (3:14) of the Holy Bible.
This is God telling Moses what to tell the Israelites and who sent Moses to them.
After the letters of W and H of the English alphabet, there are two letters of O
from the English alphabet.
This represent the relationship of the Son and the Father.
A perfect circle and a representation of the endless infinite possibilities of our
interactions with both The Null Void and God's Eternal Flame.
The letter O of the Enlish alphabet also represents the wheel and/or circle.
Without the wheel, we as a species will not be here today because everything is
moved and transported by circles (AKA wheels) in ours lives across the world.

Reference internet sources of this phrase:
https://biblehub.com/exodus/3-14.htm
https://hebraicthought.org/meaning-of-gods-name-i-am-exodus/

Reference of the letter O in the English alphbet and its symbolism of the infintie:
https://paws.kettering.edu/~lgawarec/The%20circle%20as%20symbols.pdf

The three letters (3) the word WHO in the English language is representing the three
parts of the One on Most High.
The Holy Ghost, The Son and The Father.

This represents the Catholic theological concept known as the Holy Trinity.

Three (3) is a very important number in the Holy Bible
and in other belief systems like Hatian Voudu with the head lwa known as Papa Legba.

It is also known by its common spelling Voodoo in Western/US popular cuture.

It also appears 467 times throughout the Holy Bible.

When a man and woman marry,
God is the third party that is part of the marriage and union
of two (possibly three [3]) becoming one spirit mind and flesh.

The Null and The Void coincide plus collaborate with the guiding flash of God's
Eternal Flame to strengthen those who seek the path of ever-lasting Grace.
But Blinding those who drop into orbit of the united co-existance of The Null Void.

Reference internet sources of the number Three (3) for the Holy Bible:

https://www.biblestudy.org/bibleref/meaning-of-numbers-in-bible/3.html
https://www.christianity.com/wiki/bible/what-is-the-significance-of-the-number-3-in-
the-bible.html

Reference internet sources for Papa Legba:

https://www.nps.gov/afbg/learn/historyculture/legba.htm
https://symbolsage.com/who-is-papa-legba/

Three is also the sides of a triangle.

Next to the arch, it is The most strongest stable structure know in many fields
of science and construction. Along with other related career fields like
engineering.

SAVI HEAR:

Savior

The Messiah.
The saving warmth light and grace of God's Eternal Flame.

ALMS WAYs IN U R S I N:

Always in your sin

No matter how much we try or attempt to escape the vastness of The Null Void,
the sins of being in The Null Void prevent us. Nay..... That hinder us
to our given abilities to abide by the laws that guide us to the safety of God's
Eternal Flame.

M I S S THE M A R K:

Miss The Mark

Living in sin is missing the mark or target.
Sin is the Hebrew word hhatah (חטאה) for miss the mark.
The name Mark means hammer.
The hammer (us) always misses the mark due to our sinful fallen rebellious nature
since the fall of the first humans (Adam and Eve) at the Garden of Eden.
The mark is God's overall plan for us and for all of His creation to bask in the
glow of His Eternal Flame.
The name Mark also has been known to mean Mars-like or servent.
However, the source and the mentioned two meanings in the above sentence of this
name is not clear.

Reference internet sources of the hebrew word sin:
https://www.ancient-hebrew.org/definition/sin.htm

Reference internet sources of the name Mark and Mark in the Holy Bible:

https://bibleproject.com/blog/mark-gospel-servant-messiah/
https://www.abarim-publications.com/Meaning/Mark.html

be in m ee U be e e e e e e e e e e e   f r e e e d:

Be in me, you be freed.

The letter E in the English alphabet is shown twelve (12) times after the letter in
the English alphabet B.
This is representing the Twelve (12) tribes of Israel and Judah in the Holy Bible.

The letter E in the English alphabet is shown seven (7) times after the letters in
the English alphabet F and R accordingly.
Seven is shown in the Holy Bible numerous times throughout its pages and throughout
many part of the Holy Bible.
It represents completion perfection and the holiness of God's character wisdom and
His Overall Plan.
It is known as the repersenting number of God Himself.
It also repersents the seventh (7th) day which God rested from making all creation
from the formless Null Void.
The letter E in the English alpabet is also the most common and used letter in the
English alpabet.
Representing the omniessence and omnipresence of God's Eternal Flame.

Laid on its back (|_|_|), the letter E of the English alphabet represents the
three pillars of the Holy Trinity.
The Holy Trinity is the represention of The Father The Son and The Holy Spirit.
When closed (/_|_\ ) the letter E shows the shape of two triagles connected to
the center pillar of God's Eternal Flame.
It also represents the trident. A very well known weapon symbol and tool found
throughout the nations of The Null Void.
It is also found in many myths folklores cultures and legends throughout the world
of the The Null Void.
Namely Poseidon the anicent Greek God of the Seas.
The Ψ Symbol is also the greek letter for Psi.
Which is the relationship to ESP, telepathy and psychic ablilities.
It is also the symbol of the field of psychology.
Psi is the twenty-third letter of the Greek alphabet.

Reference internet sources of the symbolism of tridents the myths of Poseidon using
tridents and its relationship to the Greek letter Psi:
https://symbolsage.com/symbolism-of-a-trident/
https://www.gfinityesports.com/fortnite/how-to-have-a-trident-symbol-in-your-fortnit
e-username-pc/
https://lerna.courses/psychology-symbol-psi-trident-greek-text-images/
https://www.britannica.com/topic/Poseidon
https://mythologysource.com/poseidons-symbol/

Reference internet source of the Greek Alphabet:
https://www.ancient-symbols.com/greek-alphabet

Reference internet sources about God, the Holy Bible and related importance of the number seven (7):

https://sevensinthebible.com/list-of-sevens-in-the-bible/
https://www.crosswalk.com/faith/bible-study/why-is-number-7-so-important-in-the-bible.html

For o l d t i m e s s a k e :

For old times sake.

Jeremiah Chapter Six Verse Sixteen (6:16) in the Holy Bible says:

Thus saith the LORD, Stand ye in the ways, and see, and ask for the old paths,
where is the good way, and walk therein, and ye shall find rest for your souls.
But they said, We will not walk therein.

Even though the modern ways are shiny and new, they are unproven paths through the
chaos and discord of The Null Void.
So stick to the old tried and true paths towards God's Eternal Flame.
They will always guide us through the confusing darkness and frustrating emptiness
of The Null Void to the flickering crackling firey source of God's Eternal Flame.

Reference internet sources of Jeremiah 6:16 in the Holy Bible:

https://biblehub.com/kjv/jeremiah/6-16.htm
https://biblia.com/bible/esv/jeremiah/6/16

AGE OF SIN AND DEATH:
The end of the age of sin and death.

The return of mighty firey wraith of God's Eternal Flame will end the age of sin and
death.
Ending the Age of Adam. By doing so, this will help germinate seeds which need the
licking touch of heat from God's Eternal Flame to form new growth. Plus provide a
new foundation
for new creation to be built upon.
The end of First Man who was tempted by the lies of those who dwelled in The Null
Void.
Who (Adam) then after eating the forbidden fruit of the knowledge of good and evil
(with his wife Eve), fell away from the caring warmth and guidance of God's Eternal
Flame.

r ood n d in our bodies our spirits and our brains:

Rotting our bodies our spirits and our brains.

Sin's detrimental rotting effect on our bodies our spirits and our brains.
The physical housing of our minds. The small yet highly important pineal gland is
rumored to be the source of all abilites of telepathy psychic astral projections and
related ESP ablities
(Extrasensory perception) from being know as the third eye. Produces DMT (or
dimethyltryptamine), a chemical known to induce dreams and visons.

Reference internet sources of the pineal gland:
https://www.medicalnewstoday.com/articles/319882#takeaway
https://dsc.duq.edu/cgi/viewcontent.cgi?article=1075&context=duquark

OUR BRAIS:

Our Praise.

Our praise to our one and only Yahweh.
Protecting us with the power and might of God's Eternal Flame.

being d a a d amed souls:

Being Daa Damned Souls:

Being The Damned Souls:

Being the damned souls we are, we suffer the effects of the Insanity Disorder
Madness and the Chaotic influence of The Null Void.
Which The Null Void we came from, which we return to and where we will remain after
The Judgement of God's Eternal Flame.
When we traverse through The Null Void, we become purified shaped and changed.
Saved and guided by the bright shining beacon of God's Eternal Flame.

If we wander lost while we adventure across The Null Void, we become damaged
misshapen hardened and deranged.
Blinded by the rage and frustration of never able to see God's Eternal Flame.
Instead, we are swept out by the every changing Chaotic Discorded Dystopian nature
of The Null Void.
With its Sirens singing out our names. To our ends we will remain.

To suffer the Second Death by the hands of The Null Void after the end (separation)
of our employment (physical or bodily end of dwelling in our temporary vessels used
to navigate around
in the planes and/or realms of The Null Void) to The Old Man (The Flesh).
Also known as The Piercing of The Veil of The Null Void.

OR

To praise The Most High with our presence being among the flickering warmth of God's

Eternal Flame.
Which is full of Everlasting Life with the Wisdom Power Beauty Awesomeness and
Strength who no one can understand or comprehend.
Let alone control and/or tame.
To the relationship we had with His All-Understanding Patient Loving Compassionate
Grace during
our existance wandering The Null Void planes.

b e d i s Grace in the Void:

Be dis Grace in the Void.

Be the Grace in The Void which you came from and which you will return to after your
existance in The Null Void planes.
After your trials and tribulations in The Void in the presence of The Old Man, this
where you go and always will remain.
Standing forever Among God's Eternal Everlasting Flame.

Notes From The Author, Shoutouts and My Background:

Since I have a few more pages to fill up before being able to have this work published into a book, I will go into my background and share what my life has been about.

I have been interested in Christianity and religion as far as I could remember.

As a yong boy going to Catholic school out in the small town in Ottawa County of Northwest Ohio.

I thank my mother and father for providing my twin and I the ability to read at a very young age.

The library was a family event and books were always a source of enlightenment entertainment and education as far as I can remember.

Whenever I found a book I stopped what I was doing and started reading whatever knowledge those pages had for me to absorb instead.

It has been the best cheering skill I have every learned
in my life.

It has been a launch pad for many many conversations and
encounters in my life.

I hope it will blast me (and others) off to many other worlds
for the many years to come.

Computers were a source of amusment and education as well.

The first few years when I was able was spent playing games
on the Commodore 64 and learning how to type.

However... as time moved on and computers improved....

AOL came online back in the 90's and dail up internet was a
sewer of information and acts of mischief.

For some time punting and lagging people online as a script kiddie was something I thought was amusing as ever. The art some of these laggers had were ahead of their time.

However, AOL didn't find this behavior as something they approved of in their TOS.

So they terminated our service and so we went to play the NES and the Game Genie instead.

We were raised around many pets and animals on that one acre of land out there. Birds were especially the ones we liked having around.

We also had cats and dogs. A gerbil and some guine pigs.

I learned how to play the horn and to read music.

I did tae kwon do with my brother.

Spent time at Clearwater Quarry and Cedar Point in Sandusky Ohio.

Camped outside in the yard while bouncing off the air mattress.

However, we moved to Toledo Ohio after the layoffs at the local nuclear plant in Ottawa County Ohio.

I learned about nuclear power from my father and other modern infrastructure that he knew about as a electrician, planner and water plant operator.

Systems we take for granted and that makes our lives easier in many of ways.

I have traveled many places in the US.

Especially to the Southwestern state of Nevada and lived in the wolrd (in)famous city of Lost Wages.... err... Las Vegas.

I am just glad Brittny Spear's songs aren't one hit wonders

anymore on the Greyhound.

Yeah she could sing and it usually it is the beat that counts.

Doesn't mean everyone who listens to it else can.

Kentucky was where I learned about ESP atral projection and other things that existed in the unseen realms of our

world.

AKA The Null Void.

It was also my starting decent into darkness, have encounters with things that one would only heard about from horror films. Plus a really messed up James Bond Dr Evil version of Voldemort.

To the bastard who said we were suppose to meet while I was there.......

I hope karma got the best of you.

But also maybe helped me realize that I needed that meeting for what I was suppose to learn many many decades later. So there's that.

To that cab driver in Seattle WA area who said what I have is a gift, not a curse when I didn't say anything to her when I got in her taxi?

Yeah, thanks for the words of encouragement understanding and wisdom that I would offer to anyone today who is hopelessly wondering the dark chaotic maddening abyss of The Null Void.

So dear reader....

Your life, situation, relationship, etc. etc... is not a curse but a gift from God above.

You cannot grow without being in this world and in the vessel given to you for overall development of His overall plan.

It will take time, but that light from God's Eternal Flame will brighten the inner halls of your life.

Changing it for the better and others around you.

To person I met on the bus while living in Vegas telling me that even though there are other realms and time lines that are better, my time and place is here.

So dear reader...

Even though you like to be into a different time and place... your time and place is here.

It will take time to understand this concept.

But evenutally you will arrive at this same conclusion as I did.

The biggest shout out I have to anyone that I have met in my life is to Danny Mendoza.

An eldery Filipino immigrant who was full of life and loved boxing.

He worked at the MGM Resort and Casino.

While I was living on the streets of Vegas looking for work, he and I met met at the bus stop on East Tropicana Ave in front of his apartment complex.

He and I talked for a little bit. Gave me his number and said to call him when I need a place to stay.

Being stubborn, I refused for a few days until I didn't have any money for a motel.

While laying on the stones of perfect desert landscape,

I thought of what I was doing and why I was being stupid sleeping outside when I had someone who wanted to help me get on my feet.

So I gave him a call and he helped me out.

Told me many stories of the people he helped through out his life in Vegas.

The methanol candies he had from the Asian Mart across the

street of his apartment was addicting as ever.

Munched on them like they were air.

Great cook too.

After about two years, I went back to Toledo Ohio to live with my father.

After a several years, I called Danny one last time.

He wasn't the cheery lively person I knew.
He complained about Vegas being hot and boring.
Then hung up.

After a few months of calling his number, I wasn't getting

anyone picking up on the other side.

I broke down and cried when I relized he wasn't going to answer the phone because I didn't get a chance to say thank you and goodbye.

To those who knew him and who he supported with a room and place to stay until they got up on their feet, tell him I said thank you for being an welcoming friend and host.

To my family and kids.....

I am grateful that you came into my life.

I wouldn't learned what I know today about not buying a shimmering, shining magic book of spells to clean up a room full of dust bunnies if it wasn't for you guys.

To my twin brother...

You are missed.

Especially when it comes to not having your around to celebrate our special day together when we were born into the realm of The Null Void so many decades ago.

I hope this poem will find you alive and well.

To the patients I helped while working as a healthcare

provider, I still remember the stories they shared with me

repeatedly of their lives long ago being in Japan after the atom
bombs were dropped.

When they were unable to recall five minutes of flipping the
channel to Rambo First Blood and saying that I wanted to
watch it with them. Baseball is pastime anyone can follow.

And of course me being the devil when one patient attempted
to knock me with his walker.

Luck of the Buddha I guess.

And last but not least my father........

I wouldn't been able to been to the places or done the things I
have done without your financial support.

I hope you find whatever God intends you to find in order to finally be happy.

I also hope He helps you become filled with joy positivity
friends family and peace in your golden years.

Sincerly,

   Michael Bartley

chaseNscores

     13boards

         Never 13e 130red.

<u>*Notes From The Author, Shoutouts and My Background:*</u>

Since I have a few more pages to fill up before being able to have this work published into a book, I will go into my background and share what my life has been about.

I have been interested in Christianity and religion as far as I could remember.

As a yong boy going to Catholic school out in the small town in Ottawa County of Northwest Ohio.

I thank my mother and father for providing my twin and I the ability to read at a very young age.

The library was a family event and books were always a source of enlightenment entertainment and education as far as I can remember.

Whenever I found a book I stopped what I was doing and started reading whatever knowledge those pages had for me to absorb instead.

It has been the best cheering skill I have every learned in my life.

It has been a launch pad for many many conversations and encounters in my life.

I hope it will blast me (and others) off to many other worlds for the many years to come.

Computers were a source of amusment and education as well.

The first few years when I was able was spent playing games on the Commodore 64 and learning how to type.

However... as time moved on and computers improved....

AOL came online back in the 90's and dail up internet was a sewer of information and acts of mischief.

For some time punting and lagging people online as a script kiddie was something I thought was amusing as ever. The art some of these laggers had were ahead of their time.

However, AOL didn't find this behavior as something they approved of in their TOS.

So they terminated our service and so we went to play the NES and the Game Genie instead.

We were raised around many pets and animals on that one acre of land out there. Birds were especially the ones we liked having around.

We also had cats and dogs. A gerbil and some guine pigs.

I learned how to play the horn and to read music.

I did tae kwon do with my brother.

Spent time at Clearwater Quarry and Cedar Point in Sandusky Ohio.

Camped outside in the yard while bouncing off the air mattress.

However, we moved to Toledo Ohio after the layoffs at the local nuclear plant in Ottawa County Ohio.

I learned about nuclear power from my father and other modern infrastructure that he knew about as a electrician, planner and water plant operator.

Systems we take for granted and that makes our lives easier in many of ways.

I have traveled many places in the US.

Especially to the Southwestern state of Nevada and lived in the wolrd (in)famous city of Lost Wages.... err... Las Vegas.

I am just glad Brittny Spear's songs aren't one hit wonders

anymore on the Greyhound.

Yeah she could sing and it usually it is the beat that counts.

Doesn't mean everyone who listens to it else can.

Kentucky was where I learned about ESP atral projection and other things that existed in the unseen realms of our

world.

AKA The Null Void.

It was also my starting decent into darkness, have encounters with things that one would only heard about from horror films. Plus a really messed up James Bond Dr Evil version of Voldemort.

To the bastard who said we were suppose to meet while I was there.......

I hope karma got the best of you.

But also maybe helped me realize that I needed that meeting for what I was suppose to learn many many decades later. So there's that.

To that cab driver in Seattle WA area who said what I have is a gift, not a curse when I didn't say anything to her when I got in her taxi?

Yeah, thanks for the words of encouragement understanding and wisdom that I would offer to anyone today who is hopelessly wondering the dark chaotic maddening abyss of The Null Void.

So dear reader....

Your life, situation, relationship, etc. etc... is not a curse but a gift from God above.

You cannot grow without being in this world and in the vessel given to you for overall development of His overall plan.

It will take time, but that light from God's Eternal Flame will brighten the inner halls of your life.

Changing it for the better and others around you.

To person I met on the bus while living in Vegas telling me that even though there are other realms and time lines that are better, my time and place is here.

So dear reader...

Even though you like to be into a different time and place... your time and place is here.

It will take time to understand this concept.

But evenutally you will arrive at this same conclusion as I did.

The biggest shout out I have to anyone that I have met in my life is to Danny Mendoza.

An eldery Filipino immigrant who was full of life and loved boxing.

He worked at the MGM Resort and Casino.

While I was living on the streets of Vegas looking for work, he and I met met at the bus stop on East Tropicana Ave in front of his apartment complex.

He and I talked for a little bit. Gave me his number and said to call him when I need a place to stay.

Being stubborn, I refused for a few days until I didn't have any money for a motel.

While laying on the stones of perfect desert landscape,

I thought of what I was doing and why I was being stupid sleeping outside when I had someone who wanted to help me get on my feet.

So I gave him a call and he helped me out.

Told me many stories of the people he helped through out his life in Vegas.

The methanol candies he had from the Asian Mart across the

street of his apartment was addicting as ever.

Munched on them like they were air.

Great cook too.

After about two years, I went back to Toledo Ohio to live with my father.

After a several years, I called Danny one last time.

He wasn't the cheery lively person I knew.
He complained about Vegas being hot and boring.
Then hung up.

After a few months of calling his number, I wasn't getting

anyone picking up on the other side.

I broke down and cried when I relized he wasn't going to answer the phone because I didn't get a chance to say thank you and goodbye.

To those who knew him and who he supported with a room and place to stay until they got up on their feet, tell him I said thank you for being an welcoming friend and host.

To my family and kids.....

I am grateful that you came into my life.

I wouldn't learned what I know today about not buying a shimmering, shining magic book of spells to clean up a room full of dust bunnies if it wasn't for you guys.

To my twin brother...

You are missed.

Especially when it comes to not having your around to celebrate our special day together when we were born into the realm of The Null Void so many decades ago.

I hope this poem will find you alive and well.

To the patients I helped while working as a healthcare

provider, I still remember the stories they shared with me

repeatedly of their lives long ago being in Japan after the atom
bombs were dropped.

When they were unable to recall five minutes of flipping the
channel to Rambo First Blood and saying that I wanted to
watch it with them. Baseball is pastime anyone can follow.

And of course me being the devil when one patient attempted
to knock me out with his walker.

Luck of the Buddha I guess.

And last but not least my father........

I wouldn't been able to been to the places or done the things I
have done without your financial support.

I hope you find whatever God intends you to find in order to finally be happy.

I also hope He helps you become filled with joy positivity friends family and peace in your golden years.

Sincerly,

   Michael Bartley

chaseNscores

     13boards

        Never 13e 130red.